The Pop Concert

...blished by Red Fox in the Read-Alone series

The Trouble With Herbert
Herbert Saves the Day
by Heather Eyles

Trouble Next Door
Philomena Hall and the Great Gerbil Caper
by Roy Apps

Henry's Most Unusual Birthday
by Elizabeth Hawkins

Cosmic Cousin
by Nancy Hayashi

My Kid Sister
by E. W. Hildick

Cat's Witch
Cat's Witch and the Monster
Tracey-Ann and the Buffalo
by Kara May

Fat Stan and the Lollipop Man
by Stephen Pern

I Want to be on TV
by Penny Speller

Stanley Makes it Big
by John Talbot

Dad's Camel
by Joan Tate

Blue Magic
Amos Shrike, the School Ghost
Snakes Alive!
Through the Witch's Window
by Hazel Townson

Mr Parker's Autumn Term
by Nick Warburton

The Pop Concert
Lily and Lorna
by Jean Wills

Rolf and Rosie
by Robert Swindells

JEAN WILLS

The Pop Concert

Illustrated by Stephanie Harris

RED FOX

A Red Fox Book

Published by Random House Children's Books
20 Vauxhall Bridge Road, London SW1V 2SA

A division of Random House UK Ltd
London Melbourne Sydney Auckland
Johannesburg and agencies throughout the world

First published by Andersen Press Ltd 1992

Red Fox edition 1993

Printed and bound in Great Britain by
Cox & Wyman Ltd, Reading, Berkshire

RANDOM HOUSE UK Limited Reg. No. 954009

ISBN 0 09 973840 6

Contents

To my family

1
Early One Morning

Early one morning the sun came over the chimney pots. Alicia looked at it so long the room was covered in yellow spots. Rubbing her eyes she rolled out of bed.

She went out of the attic at the top
of the house to the second floor, and
pushed open a door.

Pa was smiling in his sleep. Ma's
long hair played over the pillow.
Alicia watched them for a bit, then
ran on down.

In a room on the first floor Uncle
Lenny was snoring. Long drum rolls.
Breathe in and... *BRRRRHHHH!*
Breathe in and... *BRRRRHHHH!*
Alicia put her hands over her ears
and peered round his door.

She pulled a face and went quickly, down to the ground floor.

Here slept Gramp, bald as a cymbal. And Gram who smiled in her sleep like Pa. There were two pairs of teeth, in two jars of water, and they were smiling too.

'Good morning, Teeth,' said Alicia.
Gram's face began to come to life
with little twitches and starts.

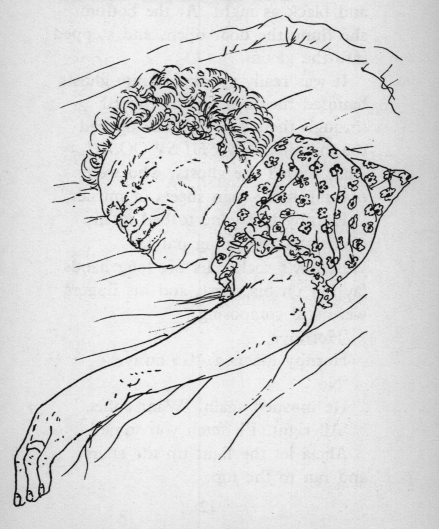

There was only one person left.

Alicia felt her way down the basement stairs. They were narrow, and black as night. At the bottom she flung the door open, and stepped into the gloom.

It was really spooky. White ghosts haunted the floor. Alicia rushed through them bravely. She opened the curtains. *SWISH! SWOOSH!* That settled the ghosts, who were nothing more than sheets of music.

Hornby had gone to bed in his clothes. A foot hung out in yesterday's sock. His big long hands lay flat on his chest, and his fingers were still composing.

'Hornby?'

Hornby moaned. 'Go away.'

'No.'

He moaned again. 'Want coffee.'

'All right. I'll fetch you some.'

Alicia let the light up the stairs, and ran to the top.

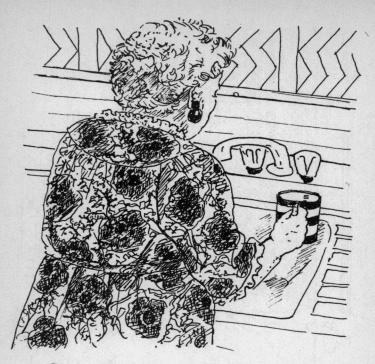

Gram was up, tied like a parcel in her summer dressing-gown. She let Alicia jerk the cord on the kitchen blinds. *SNIP! SNAP!* In came the sun.

'Hornby wants coffee, Gram. And he needs tidying.'

'Has he been composing?'

'All night, by the looks of things.'

'That Hornby. Leaves everything until the last minute.'

Gram made fresh coffee, and Alicia returned to the basement. She tidied five dirty coffee mugs, seven pencils with the ends bitten off, and thirteen chocolate wrappings. The sheets of music she piled on top of Hornby.

Hornby groaned. He opened his eyes, one at a time. Drank his coffee. And set about the sheets of music.

'All your hair is standing on end,' Alicia told him. 'Your head looks like a hedgehog.'

'*Never mind that. WHAT HAVE YOU DONE WITH IT?*'

'Done with what?'

'*My last sheet. The only one that matters, and you've lost it!*'

'Keep your hair on.'

'*NEVER MIND MY HAIR!*'

Alicia dived under the bed. There she found another mug, another pencil, and a sheet of music.

Hornby grabbed it. He clapped a large hand to his head.

'*My nerves won't stand it. ALL THIS TIDYING!*'

'If it hadn't been for me,' Alicia said huffily, 'you'd never even have found it. Whatever it is.'

She went and looked.

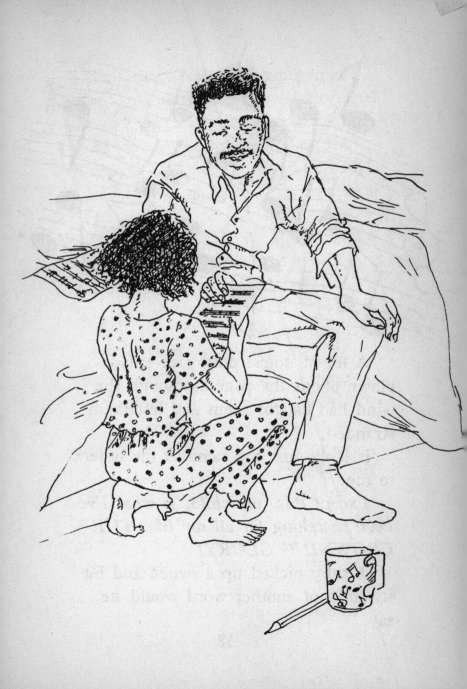

A lot of notes, dots with tails, blown about the page as though the wind had caught them and left them stranded.

'It looks just the same as the others to me.'

'Except this, my child, is what I've been searching for all my life. THE CROWNING GLORY!'

Hornby picked up a pencil and bit it, and not another word would he say.

Gramp woke next, and reached for his teeth. Alicia looked away. She didn't mind them in or out, but couldn't stand them coming or going.

'Specs,' Gramp said.

Alicia propped them on his nose.

'Mind my ears!'

'Sorry.'

'Where's my toast then?'

Gramp was allowed breakfast in bed. Alicia sat on his pillow and helped him eat it.

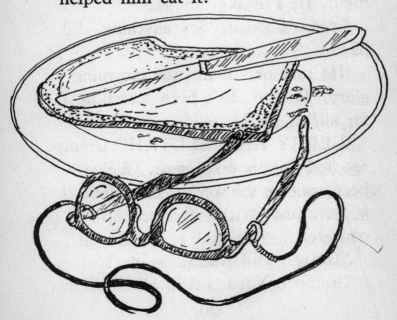

When the toast had all gone Gramp gave a great big stretch.

'No school today?'

'Of course not,' Alicia told him. 'It's the middle of the summer holidays.'

'So it is.' He frowned and listened. 'Nobody else up yet?'

'Only me and Gram.'

'What about Hornby?'

'Hornby's been composing all night. He's awake though.'

Gramp nodded. 'Say anything, did he?'

'He said he's found the crowning glory. The one he's been searching for all his life.'

'GLORY HALLELUYAH!' Gramp reached for his saxophone. 'We've been waiting for weeks. He's done it at last. Just in time for the pop concert.'

'Today?' said Alicia.

Gramp nodded, licked all round his

20

lips, and BLEW.

When he stopped Alicia said, 'I've never been to a pop concert.' She looked at the sun which covered the room with gold all over. 'I'm tired of always having to stay behind with Gram. Let me come too. OH PLEASE, GRAMP!'

2
Dear Little Buttercup

'Who am I to say?' said Gramp. 'Go ask the boss lady.'

Gram said, 'No, Alicia, certainly not.'

Alicia set to work. After ten OH

GRAMs, and twenty PLEASEs, Gram said, 'Well, we'll have to see.' And that, as everyone knows, meant that Alicia was as good as there.

To make quite certain she promised to do the washing-up when breakfast was over.

'Well, I suppose it had to come sooner or later. And it is a daytime concert, in the open air.'

'OH GRAM!'

Alicia rushed at the dressing-gown covered in red summer poppies, and put her arms round as far as they would go.

'Now get off and fetch the Band,' Gram said.

Alicia flew up to the second floor.

Pa was in the shower. Drops of water flew over the curtain. One of them landed on Alicia's nose.

'Pooh!' She shook it off.

'Is that you, my love?' Pa warbled.

'No, it's me,' Alicia said. 'And

you'll never guess. I'M COMING TO
THE POP CONCERT!'

Pa's head popped out of the
curtain. 'Who says?'

'Gram says.'

Pa was so surprised he dropped the
soap. Alicia threw it back over the
curtain.

'*Ow!*' Pa yelled. '*That was my toe!*'

'Oh dear,' said Alicia, but she was
laughing really.

She went in search of Ma.

Ma was up in the attic. Sitting by the window, in the sun, drying her crinkled hair.

'I'M COMING TO THE POP CONCERT!'

Ma shook her head.

'But I am, I AM! Gram says so. Because it's in the daytime, in the open air.' Alicia told Ma about Hornby's crowning glory. Then Ma smiled. 'Can I comb your hair?' asked Alicia.

Ma nodded. She had to save her voice for later. And now there'd be Hornby's new number as well to learn for the afternoon.

Alicia drew the big comb through Ma's long hair. She loved to pull it straight, then let the crinkles jump back. While she combed and combed Ma looked over the chimney tops. A pigeon cooed, and some sparrows flew by. It was very peaceful.

Then Gram's voice filled the house, from bottom to top.

'BREAKFAST! LAST CALL!'

'Oh help! I clean forgot!' said Alicia. 'I'm supposed to be fetching everybody.'

She hurried down to the first floor. The snores had stopped, but it was far too quiet. She thumped on Uncle Lenny's door.

'I've been sent,' Alicia shouted. 'It's BREAKFAST, LAST CALL!'

Nothing happened, so she turned the handle and looked inside.

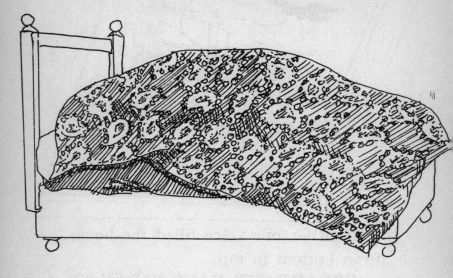

Uncle Lenny was not to be seen.
But his brown and white duvet was
all puffed up, like a chocolate éclair.

'Listen,' Alicia told the éclair.
'Hornby's composed a crowning
glory. And I'M COMING TO THE
POP CONCERT!'

Still nothing happened.

Alicia climbed on to the end of the
bed, and jumped up and down.
Uncle Lenny rose like a giant. He
roared like a giant, and Alicia ran.

She met Hornby, halfway up the basement stairs. 'I'M COMING TO THE POP CONCERT TO HEAR YOUR CROWNING GLORY!'

'Pull the other one,' Hornby said.

'No, it's true!'

After breakfast the house throbbed from basement to attic.

Uncle Lenny's drums...

Boop-da-da-da-da-da-da-Boop.

Gramp's saxophone . . . *Boo-Bah-Vee-Bee.*

Pa's bass . . . *Boomp-ba-Boomp-Boomp.*

Hornby's fingers all over the piano . . . *Bo-bi-bo-ba-bo-bi-bo-ba.*

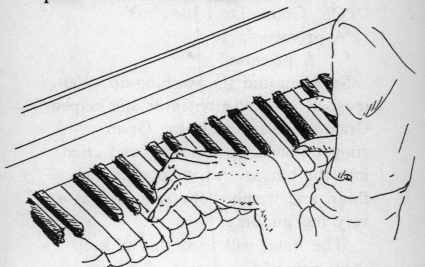

Ma's voice . . . *Be-ba-boo-ba-be-ba-boo-bah.*

'What about that washing-up?'
Gram said to Alicia.

'Oh, Gram. Do I have to?'

'A promise is...?'

'...A promise.'

So Alicia did the washing-up. Well, most of it. And afterwards she helped Gram make the pudding. Gram chopped steak and kidney, and cried into the onions. Alicia spooned the flour, and weighed the suet. It was a very big pudding.

'The Band will need this to keep them going,' Gram said. 'They've a long hard day ahead of them. And so have we.'

While the steak and kidney pudding was cooking Alicia and Gram had a kitchen concert.

Gram put the tea-cosy on her head. She lined up eight tumblers, one for each note. Then she poured in the water. The first was nearly full. The next had a little bit less, and so on,

up to the last which hardly had any.
When she'd got it right Gram played
a scale.

Alicia wore the drying-up cloth,
and blew down empty bottles.

'*All set, my beauty?*' Gram waved
her spoon.

Alicia nodded.

'*A-one, two, three!*' Gram began
her favourite song. '*Dear little
Buttercup...*'

Alicia blew. When her mouth tickled too much she sang instead, '*Dear little Buttercup...*'
Sometimes she changed to, '*Soppy old Buttercup...*'

Now and then they stopped for breath. Or to have a laugh. Put on the vegetables. Look in the oven. Lay the table. Listen for the Band...

'We're as good as they are, aren't we?'

'MUCH better,' Gram told Alicia. 'Far more of a treat.'

At dinnertime Alicia was sent to fetch the Band.

They all came and sat round the kitchen table. Hot. Weary. Gasping. STARVING.

'And how was the crowning glory?' Gram asked.

Hornby looked down at his long lean hands. Everybody else looked at one another. Then Gramp nodded and said, 'It was FINE.'

'GLORY HALLELUYAH!' Gram picked up her concert spoon and plunged it into the pudding. Out poured steam, and the yummy smell of steak and kidney. Alicia helped serve the vegetables.

When the pudding was all gone, every bit, there was Gorgonzola cheese to follow. But Ma and Alicia ate tinned peaches, which slithered nicely down their throats.

Afterwards the van was loaded. In went all the instruments. Then the people. Gram, Gramp, Pa, Ma in her silver dress, Uncle Lenny, Hornby, and for the very first time...ALICIA.

3

The Cow Cow Boogie

They drove to the other side of town.
Every time the traffic lights turned
red Uncle Lenny did drum rolls on
the steering wheel.
BRRRRRRHHHHHH...went his
fingers.

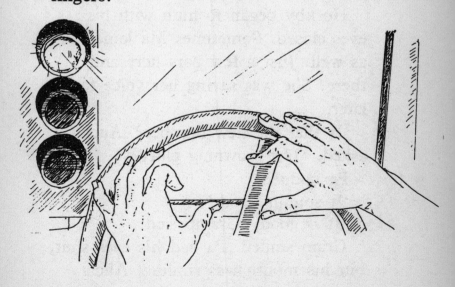

Hornby complained.

'Cool it. I'm trying to catch a nap.'

'Night is the time for sleep,' said Uncle Lenny.

'If I had slept last night you'd never have got your new number.'

The van picked up speed as Uncle Lenny drove on to the motorway.

'Will we be late?' Alicia asked.

'Not if Lenny can help it.' Gramp shut his eyes so he couldn't see the country rushing by.

Hornby began to hum with his eyes closed. Sometimes Ma joined in as well. Just a few bars here and there. She was saving her voice for later.

'Is that the new number?' Alicia asked. 'The crowning glory?'

Pa nodded.

'It sounds good.'

'It *is* good,' Gramp said.

Gram smiled. Pa had his eyes shut, but his mouth was smiling. Alicia

thought they must all be the happiest
people in the whole world.

By now they'd left the motorway
and the roads grew smaller and
smaller. They turned into such a
narrow lane that the van filled it up.
Hedges brushed against their sides.
Alicia had never seen anything like it.
The van turned a corner
and... STOPPED DEAD.

Everything shook. Van. People.
Instruments. *What a jangle!*
Everyone's eyes were wide open now.
As for Uncle Lenny, he gave the
loudest roar that Alicia had ever
heard.

She ran to the front of the van to
look over his shoulder. The lane
ahead was full of animals for as far as
she could see.

'What are they?'

'You never seen a cow before?'
Uncle Lenny roared.

'None of your temper,' Gram told Uncle Lenny. 'She's a town child.'

Alicia wanted to climb out and look, but she wasn't allowed. The van crawled on. In front moved the cows. They swung their rumps. Some of them mooed. None of them was in any hurry.

Uncle Lenny drummed his fingers, but Gramp reached for his saxophone.

'Go on,' Gram told him. 'Play *The Cow Cow Boogie.*'

So he did.

Gram sang in her funny old voice, '*...singing The Cow Cow Boogie.*'

Ma and Pa laughed, and so did Hornby. But Uncle Lenny was disgusted. He had to stop the van because the cows at the back had turned to stare.

A boy came running up from the front. He whacked the rumps of the cows at the back with a big stick.

'*Giddup!*' he cried. WHACK,

WHACK, WHACK, WHACK!
'*Giddup!*'

Alicia put her head out of the window.

'You nasty cruel thing!' she shouted.

The boy pulled a face. Then he went on whacking all the harder.

Uncle Lenny pulled Alicia inside and told her it was none of her business. But all the time she could hear outside, WHACK, WHACK, WHACK, WHACK!

'It's not fair!' Alicia said. 'All that boy does is whack the last ones.'

'They should have made sure they got up front,' Uncle Lenny said nastily.

All of a sudden Alicia could bear it no longer. She grabbed up Uncle Lenny's drumsticks, leaned out of the window and . . . WHACKED THE BOY!

He gave such a yell!

'*YEEEOWWW!*'

So did Uncle Lenny when he saw his drumsticks!

All the cows broke into a trot. They went charging along the lane and couldn't get into the field fast enough. The cowman waiting at the gate was almost knocked off his feet. Did that boy have a telling-off!

And did Alicia!

'Bringing a pest like this to a concert!' Uncle Lenny stopped the van to glare at Gram and Gramp. 'It should never have been allowed!'

'Stupid child,' Hornby said, as the van roared off again.

A tear rolled down Ma's face. It dripped on to her silver dress, and made a silver puddle. Pa put his arm round Ma's shoulders.

Alicia looked away from all of them, out of the window. If this was what coming to a pop concert was

like she wished she'd stayed at home.

The sky outside above the hedges
turned black as the kitchen stove.
Lightning ran over like boiled milk.
There was a crack of thunder, and
hailstones big as peas came down.

'The weather's angry too,' said
Gramp.

Uncle Lenny had to stop the van
again. The hailstones drummed on
top of the roof.

Gram worried about the people at the pop concert. 'They'll be soaked through in that open field.'

'Don't you believe it,' Uncle Lenny said. 'They'll all pile into their cars and drive home. *Before we even get there!*'

Alicia wanted to know about the cows.

'They can shelter under the trees,' Hornby told her. 'They don't drive cars.'

'I know that.'

'Oh, really?' said Hornby.

'Next time,' Alicia told him darkly, 'you can fetch your own coffee, and tidy yourself.'

'My brain is tidy,' Hornby replied. 'And that is all that matters.'

'You've a big fat head,' Uncle Lenny growled. 'And we might as well give up and go home.'

The windows were all steamed over. Alicia rubbed a hole and looked

out. The rain had stopped, and ahead
was a rainbow. They drove right
through it, into the sun.

'Lucky, that is,' Gram said.
'Everything will be all right now.'

'Rubbish!' roared Uncle Lenny.
But he drove on through the steaming
lanes. After a while the wetness
stopped. And when they reached the
pop concert field everywhere was dry
as a bone.

'See?' said Gram. 'That little black cloud never passed this way at all.'

Outside the air was full of music. Alicia put her head out of the window. The field sprouted...
thousands and thousands
OF PEOPLE!

Uncle Lenny sent the van bumping along the edge. People waved as they passed by, and Alicia waved back. The van stopped at the far corner behind the stage.

Hornby, Uncle Lenny, and Pa unloaded. Gramp sucked a cough lozenge. Ma sprayed her throat.

'Good luck with the new number.'
Gram gave each of them a hug in
turn. Even Uncle Lenny. AND SO
DID ALICIA.

4
End-of-the-Day Blues

The music stopped, and a band clattered off. Alicia watched her Band take its place. First Uncle Lenny, with his drums. There was a burst of clapping from the field. Next came Hornby and his keyboard. The

clapping grew louder.

'Hi, Hornby!' somebody shouted. 'Have you brought us something new?'

Hornby grinned.

'Go on, Hornby,' Alicia said. 'Tell them about the crowning glory.'

But now, as well as claps, there were cheers. Pa and Gramp were walking on. And then, her silver dress gold in the sun, came...Ma. The field went whistling wild.

Gram made Alicia go back to the van. She fetched out her big bulging knitting bag, and they sat on the tailboard.

'I'm going to make you something to remember this day by.'

'What's that?' Alicia asked.

'An End-of-the-Day jumper.'

Alicia had never heard of such a thing.

'Everything you've seen today will be knitted into it.'

'The cows? The rainbow? The field full of people?'

Gram nodded. 'All you have to do is listen...'

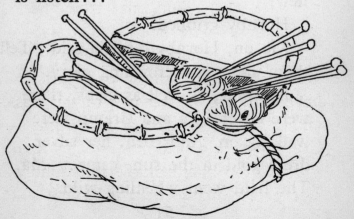

There was a loud buzz from the
microphone. The Band was ready.

'Listen to what?' Alicia said.

Hornby's hands hung over the
keyboard. Pa was ready with his bass.
Uncle Lenny scowled at his drums.
Gramp put his saxophone to his lips,
and Ma took hold of the microphone.
The people in the field fell silent.

'Just listen,' Gram said quietly.

The music began.

It was the same old stuff that Alicia had heard for ages. What was so special about that?

She slipped off the tailboard, and climbed on to the top of the van. Then she looked out over the field of people. And sang. Nobody could hear her. She couldn't even hear herself. When she got tired of singing she danced, until she almost fell off.

The music stopped, and the Band took a rest. People stood up, and some of them waved to her on the van.

Alicia waved back. Then leaned over to look at Gram.

'I think I might be getting hungry.'

'After all that pudding?'

The pudding seemed like weeks ago.

Gram threw her up a chocolate bar, an apple, and orange juice with a straw

'That's better,' Alicia said. 'Far more of a treat.'

'Now don't forget to listen...' But the Band began to play again.

After a bit Alicia lay down and watched the clouds.

'... *End-of-the-Day Blues* ...'

She opened her eyes wide. Had she
really heard those words? She listened
hard... Yes, there they were again.
Ma's voice, a little bit croaky. The
music she'd heard in the van.
End-of-the-Day Blues was Hornby's
crowning glory!

When it stopped, the people in the
field shouted, 'MORE, MORE!' As
the Band began to play again Alicia
turned back to the clouds.

The sun had gone behind the trees,
and shadow covered the van. Next
time the Band stopped Alicia couldn't
be bothered to look. There were
cloud cows walking the sky. Just like
the ones they'd followed along the
lane. *Whack, whack, whack, whack!*
But this time it was only clapping...

The van was moving!

Gram had forgotten her, and the Band hadn't noticed. Uncle Lenny had driven off with Alicia still on top! Not daring to sit up, she opened her eyes very carefully, one at a time.

She wasn't on top of the van at all, but INSIDE. Her head was on the knitting bag, and there was everybody.

Gram still knitting. The End-of-the-Day jumper had grown quite interesting. Gramp dozing. Ma and Pa, their arms round each other, fast asleep.

Hornby was up front, his great long fingers running over his knees. '*I've got those . . . End-of-the-Day Blues.*'

'Spare us,' groaned Uncle Lenny at the wheel of the van.

'It went down a treat though, didn't it?' Gram said proudly.

'Is it night-time?' Alicia asked.

'So you've woken at last.' Gram made her sit up so she could fit the jumper.

Hornby stopped singing. 'We take this child to a pop concert, and she *sleeps* through it.'

'What did I tell you?' Uncle Lenny said.

They were back inside the town, with traffic lights and lit-up houses.

'Gram,' said Alicia. 'Is *End-of-the-Day Blues* really the name of Hornby's crowning glory?'

'Yes, my beauty.'

'And my jumper?'

As Gram nodded the van drew up outside their house.

'Who's a lucky girl then?' Gramp stood up and his joints cracked. 'Oh, my poor old bones.'

When all the instruments had been taken in, Alicia climbed on Pa's back. She waved goodnight to everyone and rode up to the attic.

Ma and Pa kissed her *Good night.*
Or was it *Good morning?*

The last thing she saw before she
went to sleep was the moon over the
chimney pots.

Join the RED FOX Reader's Club

The Red Fox Readers' Club is for readers of all ages. All you have to do is ask your local bookseller or librarian for a Red Fox Reader's Club card. As an official Red Fox Reader you will qualify for your own Red Fox Reader's Clubpack – full of exciting surprises! If you have any difficulty obtaining a Red Fox Readers' Club card please write to: Random House Children's Books Marketing Department, 20 Vauxhall Bridge Road, London SW1V 2SA.

Other great reads <from **Red Fox**

Leap into humour and adventure with Joan Aiken

Joan Aiken writes wild adventure stories laced with comedy and melodrama that have made her one of the best-known writers today. Her James III series, which begins with *The Wolves of Willoughby Chase*, has been recognized as a modern classic. Packed with action from beginning to end, her books are a wild romp through a history that never happened.

THE WOLVES OF WILLOUGHBY CHASE
ISBN 0 09 997250 6   £2.99

BLACK HEARTS IN BATTERSEA
ISBN 0 09 988860 2   £3.50

THE CUCKOO TREE
ISBN 0 09 988870 X   £3.50

DIDO AND PA
ISBN 0 09 988850 5   £3.50

THE WHISPERING MOUNTAIN
ISBN 0 09 988830 0   £3.50

MIDNIGHT IS A PLACE
ISBN 0 09 979200 1   £3.50

THE SHADOW GUESTS
ISBN 0 09 988820 3   £2.99